Skye Reeds

The Courage to Let Go

Verses of Liberation and Inner Strength

Copyright © 2024 Skye Reeds. All reserved areas. No part of this book may be reproduced or transmitted in any form or by any means, electronic or mechanical, including photocopying, recording or any storage or information retrieval system, without the written permission of the author.

The Courage to Let Go

To you,
who have found the strength to turn the page,
and to anyone still searching for light along their path.
May these words be the wind beneath your wings,
guiding you toward new horizons of hope and rebirth.

Author's Note

This book is a journey.
 A journey that begins deep within pain, where the words are intimate, personal, immersed in the rawest and most real emotions.
The narrative voice speaks in the first person, reflecting the invisible scars that each of us carries within.

But there is a turning point, a moment when the pain is no longer just mine, but also yours.
From that moment on, these poems become a dialogue, addressed to you, to anyone who has experienced a difficult love, a deep wound.

This book is for those who have suffered, for those who have lost themselves but wish to find their way back.
I invite you to let yourself be guided by these words, because even when suffering feels insurmountable, there is always a way out, a path toward healing and inner freedom.

The Courage to Let Go

Chapter 1: The Darkness Before the Dawn

Chapter 2: When Love Becomes Pain

Chapter 3: Between Hope and Despair

Chapter 4: Finding the Strength Within Yourself

Chapter 5: The Courage to Let Go

The Courage to Let Go

Chapter 1: The Darkness Before the Dawn

The Courage to Let Go

The curtains are drawn,
the sun is an enemy I don't want to see.
Every breath feels like a dagger,
every thought, a torment.
You left a void I can't fill,
and this pain is devouring me alive.
My eyes are swollen with unshed tears,
too tired to cry,
too exhausted to hope.

Time moves forward, but I'm stuck,
trapped in an endless present of suffering.
I just want to close my eyes,
to silence this pain,
but death is not a solution,
it's just another way to escape.
And I'm too broken to run,
too wounded to fight.

The Courage to Let Go

The nights are the worst,
when the silence is so loud it hurts,
when memories are all I have left.
You took away my peace,
you stole my smile,
and all you left behind
is a pain I can't shake off.
Every heartbeat is a sting,
every breath feels like a burden.

The days are long,
but the nights are endless.
I just want to close my eyes,
and never open them again.
There's nothing that can fill this emptiness,
nothing that can give me my life back.
I live out of habit,
hoping that one day,
this pain will grow tired of me,
and finally leave me in peace.

The Courage to Let Go

The world has moved on,
but I'm still here,
trapped in this pain that never fades.
You took everything I had,
and left me with nothing but crumbs.
There's nothing left to hold me here,
nothing left to give me strength.

I live in the shadow of who I once was,
and every day is a struggle to survive.
I just want to close my eyes,
and never face another day without you.
But the world doesn't stop,
and I'm forced to follow it,
even though every step is torture,
even though every breath feels like a curse.

The Courage to Let Go

There is no peace in these empty rooms,
only the echo of your footsteps that will never return.
My heart is a desolate land,
barren and without hope,
and every tear is a river that dries up too soon.
I've closed the curtains to shut out the world,
to avoid seeing how it keeps spinning without you.
Time is a slow monster,
every second a blade cutting deeper.

I wish I could stop it,
freeze this pain,
but time doesn't stop,
and I remain trapped in its slow march forward.
There is no escape from this hell,
no refuge from the pain.
All I want is to sleep,
sleep until this agony becomes nothing but a faded memory.

The Courage to Let Go

The Courage to Let Go

The words have run out,
now there are only tears,
tears that flow without end,
like a river that knows no rest.
Pain is a shadow that follows me,
a weight I cannot lift.
Every memory of you is a dagger,
sinking into my flesh,
nestling in my heart.

Food has lost its taste,
life has lost its meaning.
Every moment is a waiting,
a waiting for something, anything,
that could bring relief to this torment.
But nothing comes,
nothing changes,
and here I remain,
in this darkness,
searching for an escape
that doesn't exist.

The Courage to Let Go

Your goodbye was a blow to my heart,
a strike I can't recover from.
Each day begins with new pain,
each night a battle already lost.
I can't breathe,
I can't think,
all I can do is feel,
feel this pain that's killing me.

I want to scream,
I want to tear away this suffering,
but there's no escape,
there's no way out.
All that's left is the desire,
the desire to end it all,
to bring this torment to a close.
But even that desire is just a dream,
a dream I can't afford to make real.

The Courage to Let Go

The Courage to Let Go

I am a prisoner of this pain,
a prisoner with no visible chains.
Every corner of my soul is wounded,
every breath is a battle against the tears.
Time doesn't heal,
time doesn't forgive,
time moves slowly,
while I remain trapped in this endless present.

I wish I could sleep,
I wish I could forget,
but there's no sleep deep enough,
no oblivion that can erase you.
You've left me with this emptiness,
a void I cannot fill,
and all I have left
is the hope that one day
this pain will soften,
that one day I can remember you without dying inside.

The Courage to Let Go

You made me kneel,
as if my dignity was a burden
you had to lift.
Every time you spoke,
every time you laughed at me,
I felt the fire inside me fade.
You turned every mistake of mine
into a weapon to destroy me.

You made me small,
so small that I no longer recognize myself.
Every word you said was a low blow,
and I, unable to defend myself,
watched you lower your gaze at me,
as if I were nothing,
as if I were just the reflection
of your anger.

The Courage to Let Go

I am no longer myself.
Looking in the mirror,
I see emptiness,
a reflection of who I once was,
but who no longer exists.
You erased every part of me,
one piece at a time,
until there was nothing left
but a mask,
the one I wear to keep you from getting angry.

I have no more dreams,
no more desires,
because you consumed them all,
like a fire that never stops burning.
And what have I become?
Just a shadow,
an echo of a voice that once screamed loud,
but now no longer exists.

The Courage to Let Go

You bombarded me with love,
Showered me with affection,
Sweet words, and promises you'd never keep.
At first, I thought I was special,
That I was the only one you wanted,
The only one who mattered.
But it wasn't love.
It was control, wrapped in pretty words,
Manipulation disguised as devotion.

You made me believe that without you,
I was nothing.
You filled my heart with lies,
Made me doubt my own worth,
Until I couldn't tell where you ended,
And I began.
But now I see through it all,
And I'm reclaiming myself,
Piece by piece,
From the ruins you left behind.

The Courage to Let Go

Chapter 2: When Love Becomes Pain

The Courage to Let Go

They call it love,
but love isn't supposed to feel like a cage.
Suffocating under the weight of control,
drowning in a sea of carefully crafted lies.
The need to dominate masquerades as affection,
turning tender moments into a battlefield.

It's not love, it's a war,
and I'm the one left bleeding.
In the process of saving someone else,
i lost myself.
But now, it's time to turn the focus in waitrd
and finally save me.

The Courage to Let Go

The Courage to Let Go

Once, everything was promised,
but I was merely a puppet on a string.
With each pull,
another piece of me was lost,
tethered by declarations that tightened the leash.

Clarity has struck,
there was never a desire for partnership,
Only control.
the role I played is over,
and I'm stepping off this stage,
ready to reclaim what's mine.

The Courage to Let Go

Belief in "forever" was once unwavering,
until it became an excuse for every transgression.
Apologies turned into weapons,
tears used to manipulate and bind.
My own essence drained away,
poured into the endless void within another.

But love isn't meant to hurt like this.

No longer will I be the crutch to lean on.
Walking away might shatter me,
but staying would be a slow, inevitable death.

The Courage to Let Go

You wore me down,
piece by piece,
until I couldn't see the cracks.
You called it love,
but love doesn't destroy like this.

Every kiss was a lie,
every touch a reminder of my chains.
Now, I'm breaking free,
leaving behind the ashes of what you called love.
This isn't goodbye,
It's a fucking escape.

The Courage to Let Go

Submission was cultivated,
a heart used as a shield to deflect guilt.
Every attempt to leave was thwarted,
by promises of a change that never arrived.
Chains disguised as love continued to tighten.

Now, the truth is clear,
the mask of a master manipulator has been lifted.
No longer will I be a prisoner.
I'm reclaiming what remains of me,
and breaking free from the grip that once held me captive.

The Courage to Let Go

Every laugh you made,
every glance you threw,
was a blade hidden behind smiles.
You never spoke the truth,
but you made sure my reality
was built on your lies.

Every step I took,
was like walking on barbed wire,
waiting to fall,
waiting for you to push me down.
But I won't fall anymore.
Your hands won't control me,
your poison won't stop me.
I am free, and now every blow you land falls into
emptiness.

The Courage to Let Go

Whenever I tried to speak,
you'd break my words in half,
twisting them, bending them,
until it seemed like I was the problem.
You played with my mind,
as if it were a fucking puzzle to solve.
But I wasn't some riddle to be deciphered,
I was just a person searching for love.

And you, you never knew what love was.
You used my weakness against me,
made me believe I was never enough.
But now, every piece of me you shattered,
is coming back together.
And you will never be part of my mosaic again.

The Courage to Let Go

The Courage to Let Go

You twisted every word I spoke,
changed every truth,
until I began to doubt myself.
You looked at me with contempt,
as if I was always a mistake,
always a disappointment.
Every tear I shed was a victory for you,
another sign of your triumph over me.

You bent me,
you broke me,
made me feel small, insignificant.
And when I tried to escape,
you pulled me down even harder,
like some fucking puppet in your hands.
But I am not yours anymore,
I am no longer your shadow.
My voice will scream again,
even though you silenced me for far too long.

The Courage to Let Go

You always put yourself at the center,
as if the world revolved only around you.
Every joy of mine was a threat to your ego,
every sadness,
an opportunity to inflate your vanity.
You played with my emotions,
like a puppeteer
pulling the strings just to watch me fall.

You made me believe I was the one who was wrong,
that I wasn't enough,
while you fed off my insecurity.
Your love was just a reflection,
not of me,
but of yourself.
And I, blind,
mistook that reflection for reality.
But now I see you for who you truly are:
just a shadow,
empty,
feeding on the pain of others.

The Courage to Let Go

Every word that left your mouth
was an invisible punch.
Every insult, every shout,
a blow that pushed me further down.
Your hands didn't need to wrap around my throat
to make me choke,
your gaze was enough,
that anger shining in your eyes
before you hit me.

Every time you raised your voice,
I felt myself disappear,
as if my worth was an illusion,
shattered under the weight of your words.
And then, when words were no longer enough,
your hands found a way
to make me feel the pain on my skin,
not just in my soul.

The Courage to Let Go

Chapter 3: Between Hope and Despair

The Courage to Let Go

Don't fucking give up now,
I know the shit has hit you hard,
That the darkness seems never-ending,
But there's a fire inside you,
That not even hell can put out.
You've already endured the unbearable,
You've already hit rock bottom,
But you know what?

You weren't made to stay down.
Every scar, every fucking tear,
Is proof of your resilience.
No one can extinguish your flame,
Except you.
So get the fuck back up,
This isn't your ending,
It's just the beginning of a new battle,
And this time, you're ready to win.

The Courage to Let Go

Stop crying,
That bastard broke you,
But you're not made to stay broken.
Life's hit you with some low blows,
It's knocked you down,
But here's the real question: will you give up?

Or will you get back up, with fire in your eyes,
And a "fuck you" ready on your lips?
This shit isn't meant for you,
You're made to fight,
To kick down those closed doors.
Don't let anyone tell you who you are,
You're a fucking hurricane,
And the world just needs
to learn how to respect you.

The Courage to Let Go

The Courage to Let Go

Hell isn't enough to stop you,
I know it hurts,
That the pain takes your breath away,
But you have the right to scream,
To shout against this fucked-up world.
Don't let your scars define you,
Those are the medals you've earned,
Every time you fell and got back up.

You've walked through the flames,
And you didn't burn,
You just learned to shine even brighter.
So stop listening to that voice that says "give up,"
It's nothing but fear disguised as wisdom.
Inside you is the strength of a thousand storms,
And damn, no one can stop you.

The Courage to Let Go

You've survived all of this,
Don't let a moment of weakness
Make you believe you're worth nothing.
You've walked through darkness,
You've felt the weight of the world on your shoulders,
And yet, you're still here,
Still standing, still alive.

The world has tried to bend you,
But you weren't made to break.
Every breath you take
Is an act of defiance against the shit around you.
There's nothing wrong with you,
You're a fucking warrior,
And no one can tell you otherwise.

The Courage to Let Go

Pain has taught you not to trust,
But, you can't live in suspicion forever.
Every day you wake up
Is another chance to say fuck it all,
And take your life back.
Don't let fear hold you back,
Don't let the demons of your past
Steal your future.

You've seen the worst,
You've hit rock bottom,
And yet you're still here,
Ready to fight again.
This is the moment to say enough,
To say, "fuck it, I deserve more,"
And kick the ass of anyone who tries to stop you.
You're not made to give up,
You're made to dominate,
And damn, you will.

The Courage to Let Go

You relished watching me fall, didn't you?
Each tear I shed fueled that wicked smile of yours,
like it was a personal victory.
You built your kingdom on my pain,
and I was your prisoner.

You filled every corner of my mind
with doubts, with fears,
until I could no longer recognize myself.
But now, that kingdom you built
is crumbling under the weight of your lies.
I'm walking away,
and you'll be left there,
to rule over the ruins you created.

The Courage to Let Go

The Courage to Let Go

You weren't made to stay down,
No matter how hard they tried to break you.
You've fallen before,
But every fall has made you stronger.
The weight of their words,
The blows of their lies,
They all tried to bury you,
But they didn't know what you were capable of.

You are not meant to stay in the shadows,
You were born to rise,
To shine even when the world tries to dim your light.
Every scar is a reminder of the battles you've fought,
And damn it, you're still here.
Don't let anyone tell you otherwise,
You weren't made to stay down—
You were made to conquer.

The Courage to Let Go

I was never enough, was I?
Every glance you threw at me was filled with disdain,
as if you questioned why I was there, why I existed.
You tore away my strength,
you stole my voice,
until there was nothing left but silence.

But silence, for you, was too loud,
so you kept digging,
kept striking blows to make sure
there was nothing left to save.
And I, blind and broken, thought it was my fault.
But now I know.
The real emptiness was never inside me,
it was always inside you.

The Courage to Let Go

The Courage to Let Go

You left a hole in my chest,
an emptiness I can't seem to fill,
no matter how much I scream, how much I cry.
It's like a bottomless pit,
swallowing me piece by piece.
The days pass slowly,
but inside me there's only darkness,
a storm that never stops.

Every time I try to breathe,
there's a knot in my throat that won't go away.
I just want to disappear,
because living like this isn't really living,
it's only surviving,
clinging to something that no longer exists.
You're gone,
and I am nothing without you.

The Courage to Let Go

This pain has no name,
no face,
it's just a weight I carry on my heart,
every damn day.
There's not a breath that doesn't hurt,
not a thought that doesn't lead me back to you.
If only I could stop time,
if only I could shut everything off for a moment.

But time doesn't stop,
and I am trapped,
in this life I no longer recognize,
in this existence that only brings me pain.
Every night is a lost battle,
every morning another blow.
There's no escape,
no shelter,
only this endless agony.

The Courage to Let Go

The silence is killing me,
that emptiness that fills every room,
every corner of my soul.
There are no more words,
no more promises,
just the deafening sound of your absence.
I've lost everything,
even myself.
I don't know who I am anymore,
I don't know what I want anymore.

Every step feels pointless,
every breath an immense struggle.
I wish I could forget you,
erase every memory,
but you're etched into my skin,
into my blood,
and I can't break free from you.
Pain has become my companion,
my only comfort,
because at least it makes me feel alive,
even though I don't want it anymore.

The Courage to Let Go

The Courage to Let Go

Do you remember that time you said you loved me?
I believed it, God, how I believed it.
Every one of your lies was like sweet poison,
easy to swallow.
You gave me a love that burned,
but never warmed me.
It was a trap,
a fucking deception.

And I, desperate, tried to hold on
to the little that was left.
But there was nothing.
Only empty promises you'd never fulfill.
And now, that fire that destroyed me,
has become the flame that sets me free.

The Courage to Let Go

You taught me to bend,
to silence my voice,
my will,
to make room for yours.
Every desire of mine became a fault,
every decision,
a wound to your pride.
You asked me to submit,
to erase who I was,
to become your shadow,
always one step behind you.

I lost myself in your hands,
in your unspoken rules,
as I tried to be enough
to deserve your love.
But love doesn't demand submission,
and I'm tired of being a prisoner
in my own body.

The Courage to Let Go

You told me it was love,
that you were here to save me.
But every word of yours was like a blade,
sharp, invisible, ready to strike.
You filled my life with lies,
poisonous like smoke that slowly wrapped around me,
suffocating my freedom, my breath.

You made me believe that without you
I could never exist.
But what you gave me wasn't love,
it was a slow poison,
creeping inside me,
draining every ounce of my strength,
until I no longer recognized myself.
It's not love if it kills you little by little.

The Courage to Let Go

The Courage to Let Go

In the beginning,
you were everything.
Your words were sweet like honey,
filling every empty corner of my soul.
You made me believe I was special,
that I was your queen,
while you showered me with attention,
with promises you knew you'd never keep.

Every move you made, every glance,
was calculated,
it was a trap,
and I fell for it.
You bombarded me with love,
made me believe that without you,
I would be nothing.
But true love doesn't play tricks,
it doesn't build sandcastles
that crumble at the first storm.

The Courage to Let Go

Don't let that son of a bitch put you in a corner.
You're not his rag doll,
You're not his cross to bear.
If love hurts,
then it's not love,
It's poison that's eating you from the inside.
There's nothing wrong with you,
The problem is him and his fear of losing control.

But you're too strong to let him dim your light like that.
Do yourself a favor,
Kick him the hell out of your life.
Yes, you'll cry, you'll scream,
But in the end,
you'll find peace.
Because freedom is your right,
And no man has the power to take it from you.

The Courage to Let Go

Chapter 4: Finding the Strength Within Yourself

The Courage to Let Go

How do you walk away
from something that once made your heart race?
How do you leave behind
the love that was supposed to save you,
but only chained you tighter?

The pain of letting go is so sharp,
it feels like a knife cutting deep into your soul.
But every second I stay,
I die a little more inside.
I have to let you go,
not because I'm weak,
but because I deserve more than this.

The Courage to Let Go

The Courage to Let Go

I thought I could save you,
that if I loved you enough,
you would see the light.
But loving you was like trying to hold water in my hands,
it slipped away,
leaving me empty and drenched in my own tears.

Letting you go is like tearing off a limb,
but what's left of me can finally heal.
I'll leave now,
even though it feels like I'm losing everything.
Because in truth,
I've already lost enough.

The Courage to Let Go

We held on for so long,
clinging to broken promises,
faking smiles through the cracks.
I kept hoping, praying,
that one day you would see me,
truly see me.
But I was always a reflection of your desires,
never truly myself.

The hardest part isn't leaving,
it's realizing I stayed too long.
Now, as the tears fall,
I find strength in letting go,
in the freedom of finally leaving the past behind.

The Courage to Let Go

You made me believe
that without you, I was nothing.
That my worth was tied to the love you gave me,
even though that love burned me alive.
But I've learned that real love doesn't suffocate,
doesn't destroy,
doesn't leave scars.

Letting you go is like ripping off a bandage,
it burns, it hurts,
but underneath,
I am healing.
And maybe, just maybe,
one day I'll feel whole again.

The Courage to Let Go

The Courage to Let Go

There's no easy way to walk away from love,
no simple way to say goodbye to what we built.
But love shouldn't be a battlefield,
and I'm tired of fighting.
Letting you go is the hardest thing I've ever done,
but holding on to you is destroying me.

I deserve peace,
I deserve a love that doesn't hurt.
So, with tears in my eyes and pain in my heart,
I choose to leave.

The Courage to Let Go

I never thought I'd get here,
standing on the edge of goodbye.
But sometimes love isn't enough,
sometimes the pain outweighs the joy.
I fought for us,
for you,
for the dreams we once shared.

But now, I'm fighting for myself.
Letting you go isn't weakness,
it's understanding when it's time to stop holding on
to something that's already gone.

The Courage to Let Go

I cried the day I realized you weren't coming back,
not because I missed you,
but because I finally understood
that I deserved better.
Letting go doesn't mean forgetting,
it means freeing myself from the grip you had on me,
breaking free from the chains
of a love that never really existed.
The tears will dry,
and I will rise again.

The Courage to Let Go

The Courage to Let Go

There comes a moment when you realize
that holding on hurts more than letting go.
I've reached that moment,
and now, I'm free.
The pain is still there,
but it's a different kind of pain
the kind that heals,
the kind that sets you free.
I loved you,
but now I love myself more.
And that's why I'm walking away.

The Courage to Let Go

It wasn't love,
it was a trap.
Every time I got closer,
I felt the ground crumble beneath my feet,
an abyss below me,
the emptiness of an affection that was never really there.

I've walked this tightrope for too long,
every step shaky,
every breath unsure.
And now I'm tired,
I no longer want to walk among your lies.
I'm not looking for your hand to steady me,
I'm only seeking my freedom,
the one that was stolen from me.

The Courage to Let Go

My heart was a garden,
full of flowers I tended with care.
But you,
with your harsh words,
came like a storm,
destroying every petal,
ripping away every hope.

Now my garden is barren,
just empty, dry soil.
But this silence,
this emptiness,
is the ground on which I will begin to plant myself again.
And without you,
the flowers will grow stronger than ever before.

The Courage to Let Go

The Courage to Let Go

You never truly saw who I was,
you only looked at me through the mirror of your insecurities.
Every smile I gave you,
you broke it in half.
Every hug I offered,
you let it fall to the ground like ashes.
I got lost in your eyes,
but now I see who I am,
and who I will no longer be by your side.
My reflection is smiling back at me again,
and this time, it's not you making me shine

The Courage to Let Go

The weight of us was unbearable,
it crushed me more every single day.
And I, foolish,
kept carrying it,
convinced it was normal,
that love meant sacrifice.

But the sacrifice took away my lightness,
it stole my breath,
and now I need to free myself from this burden.
I no longer seek excuses for you,
nor for us.
Now I just want to reclaim my space,
the space you invaded without asking.

The Courage to Let Go

Your hands didn't hold me,
they imprisoned me.
Every touch of yours was a chain,
a limit imposed on my soul.
You fed off my desire to be loved,
growing your ego
while my heart faded.

Now, in the quiet of this solitude,
I can feel my heart beat again.
A timid beat,
but it's the sound of my freedom.

The Courage to Let Go

The Courage to Let Go

There are nights when I still feel your breath,
those cold nights when my mind
betrays me with memories of you.
But then I wake up,
I hold myself tight,
and I remember that I survived.

You were only a chapter,
a part of my story,
but not the ending.
And as I rise again,
your traces slowly fade away,
making room for what's to come.

The Courage to Let Go

You had a sneaky way of making me feel small,
of making me believe that everything depended on you,
that without you, the world would collapse.
And yet, it collapsed right alongside you.

But from the rubble, I found a way out,
I found my courage,
the courage you always tried to extinguish.
Now I walk without chains,
without your weight on my shoulders.
You will never be my burden again.

The Courage to Let Go

The Courage to Let Go

Every time I tried to fight for us,
you made me feel like I was fighting a losing battle.
But the battle wasn't for us,
it was for my soul,
for my heart that was crying out to be saved.

And in the end, I wasn't the one who lost.
It was you.
Because I chose to fight for myself,
for my future without your chains.

You never understood what love was,
you confused control with affection,
manipulation with care.
But I'm no longer here to explain it to you.
I've found my own path,
and now I'm no longer searching for your answers.

My heart,
which once beat for you,
has found a new rhythm,
the rhythm of freedom.

The Courage to Let Go

The Courage to Let Go

I've learned that scars
are not marks of weakness,
but the map of my courage.
Every wound you left on me
has become a lesson,
a reminder of my strength.
I'm no longer ashamed of my cracks,
because through them
the light finds its way in.

The Courage to Let Go

I stopped waiting for the world to change,
I realized that the change had to start with me.
I looked in the mirror
and saw a warrior,
a woman who had weathered storms
and came out stronger.
I no longer wait for salvation,
because I've understood
that I can save myself.

The Courage to Let Go

The path to healing has not been linear.
There were days when I thought I wouldn't make it,
moments when the pain felt unbearable.
But every time I fell,
I got back up.
And each time I stood up again,
I became stronger.

The Courage to Let Go

The Courage to Let Go

Chapter 5: The Courage to Let Go

The Courage to Let Go

I found my peace
in letting go of what I couldn't control.
I stopped fighting against the wind,
and learned to dance with it.
I no longer care about winning or losing,
I only care about being free,
and finally, I am.

The Courage to Let Go

Healing is not a destination,
it's a continuous journey.
There will be dark days,
days when the past seems to drag me down.
But now I know I can face them,
I can carry the weight of my past
without letting it define my future.
I've learned that strength comes from within.
No matter how many times I fall, I will rise again.
The scars I carry tell my story, but they don't define me.

Every breath is a reminder that I survived.
I refuse to be a prisoner of my past.
Each step forward, no matter how small, is progress.
I am no longer seeking approval, I am finding my worth.
The pain shaped me, but it didn't break me.
I will not let yesterday's wounds dictate tomorrow's dreams.
I am healing, growing, and becoming who I was always meant to be.

The Courage to Let Go

The Courage to Let Go

I no longer search for happiness in others,
I no longer wait for someone to complete me.
I've realized that I'm already whole,
that I don't need to be saved.
My life is mine,
my joy is in my hands,
and I'm finally free to be
who I've always been.

I have reclaimed my power,
I have stopped apologizing for my strength.
No one else holds the key to my peace,
because I've learned to find it within.
I am no longer defined by others' expectations.
I choose my path, my pace, my truth.
And in this freedom, I am unbreakable.
This is the life I was always meant to live.

The Courage to Let Go

I stopped apologizing
for who I am,
for my dreams,
for my voice.
I will no longer try to be less
just to make others feel bigger.
I am here,
I am strong,
and I will never dim my light again
out of fear of overshadowing someone.

I have learned that my strength is not a threat,
but a gift.
I will no longer apologize for my power,
nor for my presence.
My worth is not measured by others' fragility,
but by my ability to shine without fear.
I don't need to prove anything to you,
and I don't need your approval.
From now on, I will walk with my head held high,
aware of my worth and my uniqueness.

The Courage to Let Go

The Courage to Let Go

Have you ever wondered who you would be,
without all the shit you keep inside?
Without that mask you put on every day
to seem strong,
even when you feel like you're about to break?
The problem is, you're not broken,
you've just never allowed yourself to be whole.

Have you ever had the courage to truly look at
yourself,
to face the emptiness you keep filling with silence?
Maybe you're afraid to discover
that everything you need
has always been inside you.

The Courage to Let Go

Do you know how many times I've erased myself
just to make you happy?
How many fucking times I've put aside my dreams
to avoid hurting your fragile ego?
Enough.
I'm not the missing piece of your puzzle,
I'm my own complete masterpiece.

Fuck you and your need for control.
You tried to dim my light,
but all you did was make it shine brighter.
I won't be your shadow anymore,
I won't live in your reflection.
I am everything I need to be,
without you.

The Courage to Let Go

The Courage to Let Go

Is it really love if it takes your breath away,
not because it's beautiful,
but because it suffocates you every fucking day?
Have you ever wondered
if the love you're chasing
is really what you deserve
or just what they've made you believe you deserve?

What's romantic about pain?
Why do you keep fighting for something
that's consuming you piece by piece?
Love shouldn't make you feel like a prisoner,
it should set you free.
Maybe it's time to stop searching for love in others
and start finding it within yourself.

The Courage to Let Go

There's no glory in holding on to a love
that consumes your soul.
Letting go isn't defeat,
it's liberation.
Why the fuck should you keep
carrying the weight of something
that's destroying you?
Every day you stay,
you lose a piece of yourself.

Don't call it sacrifice,
call it slavery.
You deserve a love that lifts you,
not one that drags you down.
There's no strength in enduring,
real strength is knowing when to say enough.
Letting go is an act of rebellion,
it's a cry for freedom.

The Courage to Let Go

The Courage to Let Go

Every day you wake up
and choose to keep going.
Even when every fiber of your being
screams to give it all up.
Damn, that's courage.
And don't ever let anyone tell you otherwise.
You stand tall when the world wants you broken,
and that makes you invincible, even when you don't
realize it.

Every breath, every step forward,
is a victory, even if it seems small.
Pain has bent you,
but it hasn't broken you.
Keep fighting,
because this journey is yours,
and you deserve to see where it will take you.

The Courage to Let Go

The most fucked up thing about all of this?
You were enough even before you fell,
you were already strong before the fight.
But you had to walk through the fire
to truly understand it.
Every scar you carry
isn't a sign of your weakness,
but proof that you survived.

And now, every step you take
is an anthem to your resilience.
You didn't become strong,
you've always been strong.
You just had to look inside yourself
to see how strong you really were.

The Courage to Let Go

You know what hurts the most?
Not the breakdown, but holding everything in.
Pain doesn't fade when you hide it,
it builds up and consumes you.
You feel it grow, piece by piece,
until you can't breathe anymore.

You try to smile, to pretend everything's fine,
but inside there's a storm that never stops.
And the more you try to ignore it,
the more it takes control.
The truth is, to heal,
you have to let it out,
you have to face it head-on,
even if it's terrifying.

The Courage to Let Go

Do yourself a favor:
stop waiting for someone to save you.
No one's coming,
and even if they did,
they wouldn't have the right key for you.
You have to open that door yourself.
Every day you wait,
you drift further away from yourself.

Your strength isn't hidden in someone else,
it's within you,
even if sometimes you forget how powerful you are.
You don't need a hero,
you've always been your own salvation.
Open your eyes,
and you'll see that you are more than enough.

The Courage to Let Go

I walked through the ruins of my heart,
and for a moment,
I believed there was nothing left.
But broken ground can bloom again, scars can
become fertile soil for something new.
Every tear is a seed I plant,
and from the ashes of my suffering,
I see a garden beginning to grow.
No longer just survival,
but a true blooming towards the light.

The Courage to Let Go

There is a new morning after every night,
even when the darkness feels eternal.
The sun rises without asking permission,
and so too has my heart begun to shine again.
I have allowed the light to filter through the cracks,
and now those same cracks are my pride.
It doesn't matter how many times I have fallen,
what matters is that I have always been able to get
back up.

The Courage to Let Go

I don't need anything extraordinary,
just the strength of a smile in the morning.
Just the warmth of the sun on my face,
just the promise of a better day.
I have discovered that happiness is made of small things,
those moments when the heart feels light.
And now,
I walk towards a world where inner peace is no longer a dream,
but a reality I create every day.

The Courage to Let Go

I spent too much time in the shadows,
waiting for permission to shine.
But now I see there's no need to wait,
that the light is inside me.
Even though I was broken,
even though I went through storms,
every piece of me now reflects the light,
and it's my time to shine,
without fear.

The Courage to Let Go

Even when the sky was gray and seemed endless,
I kept walking.
Clouds can't stay forever,
the sun must emerge.
And now,
after all that darkness,
I see a rainbow in my eyes.
This is the beauty of life,
the promise that after every storm,
there will always be some light.

The Courage to Let Go

My soul was tired,
broken under the weight of what had been.
But from the depths of pain,
I found the strength to be reborn.
The past taught me what it means to be fragile,
and now I've discovered what it means to be strong.
Each day is a new promise,
a new opportunity to love myself more.

The Courage to Let Go

I lost countless days drowning in the "why,"
searching for a reason behind all that pain.
But I've realized the past holds no answers,
only memories that I can't change.
The real meaning is here, in the present—
in every breath that fills my lungs.
Today, I choose to leave the questions behind,
to stop searching for reasons that don't matter anymore.

Life is still ahead of me,
unfolding with each new dawn,
and I no longer need to stay in the shadows.
I'm stepping into the light,
ready to embrace the unknown,
to live fully, and begin again.

The Courage to Let Go

There was a part of me that never stopped hoping,
even when everything seemed lost.
That part,
small and fragile,
was my beacon in the night.
I've learned that trust isn't built on certainties,
but on a deep knowing that life still has wonders to offer.
Today,
I welcome each new dawn with open arms,
believing wholeheartedly that there will always be another day to live.

The Courage to Let Go

The tears that fell have watered my soil,
and now I see the first sprouts of hope.
I am no longer the person I was,
I am something new,
something that survived the darkness and found the light.
Every scar is a mark of my journey,
every smile,
a symbol of my victory.

The Courage to Let Go

I have freed myself from the chains that held me,
the ones that kept me from dreaming.
Now, I walk with my head held high,
the wind in my hair,
and a light heart.

I know I was broken,
but I also know I have rebuilt myself.
I'm no longer afraid,
I am no longer a shadow,
I am the best version of myself,
and I am ready to live my life,
ree and whole.

The Courage to Let Go

Dear reader,

From the bottom of my heart, thank you for reading The Courage to Let Go.
Writing these poems was a deeply personal and emotional journey, filled with moments of vulnerability and acts of courage.
Every verse was born from the hope of offering comfort, understanding, and a spark of light to anyone going through a difficult time.

The fact that you took the time to read this book means so much to me.
I hope the words you found here have spoken to your soul, resonated with your experiences, and maybe even helped you find a bit of peace or strength along your own path.

If you found value in these pages, I'd like to ask you a small favor: please consider leaving a review on Amazon.

The Courage to Let Go

Your opinion means the world to me, and it can make a big difference for others as well.
Reviews help the book reach a wider audience, allowing these words to find their way to those who need them, to those searching for comfort, answers, or just a bit of understanding during dark times.

I understand how precious your time is, so I am incredibly grateful if you decide to share your thoughts and impressions.

Every word, every review, helps more than you might imagine.

With gratitude and affection,

Skye Reeds

Made in the USA
Las Vegas, NV
21 March 2025

19942925R00069